American Patriots

Presents

Gov. Ron DeSantis

I0085288

American Patriots
Presents:
Governor Ron DeSantis

Copyright © By American Patriots Publishing

business@americanpatriotspublishing.com

ISBN: 978-0-9810511-7-8

The quotations included in this book have been gathered
via copious sources (analog and digital)
and researched for authenticity and accuracy. Some
quotes collected are being presented without
context, and may therefore be imperfectly worded or attributed.
To the subject/authors, contributors and original sources,
our thanks, and where appropriate, our apologies. – The Editors

Printed in the United States of America

"We need to save the country"

"MY ACTIONS WILL SPEAK LOUDER THAN WORDS"

"

Proud to defend life!

"A limited government
is much more likely
to be
a competent
government"

"You can't just magically create subsides through executive fiat"

"Very rarely do firearms restrictions affect criminals. They really only affect law-abiding citizens."

"If Congress adds
5 percent to
the debt,
then their
pay should
be cut by 5 percent"

"

Math is about getting the right answer,
not about feelings or ideologies.
In Florida, we will be educating
our children, not indoctrinating them.

"Don't make government
work like a business
... it's inherently inefficient"

"At the end of the day, I'm fighting for the things I said I'd fight for"

"On International Holocaust Remembrance Day, we must never forget the tragedy of the Holocaust and also continue to confront antisemitism wherever it rears its ugly head"

"We need a new generation of leaders who will promote policies that will foster economic growth and alleviate the middle class squeeze, defend America's national security against those who threaten our people, reform the culture of Washington, D.C., and reassert the constitutional principles that make our country unique"

"Merely implying bias due to a judge's ethnic heritage is wrong as a matter of principle and legally illegitimate"

"

All presidents are not created equal,
and while we colloquially call today
Presidents Day, the holiday is codified
in law solely to commemorate
Washington's birthday. This is
appropriate, as Washington is
America's indispensable man.
Happy Birthday to the father of our country!

"Too many in Washington display a ruling class mentality, and congressional term limits would go a long way towards restoring the citizen-legislator ethos of the Founding Fathers"

"I was always the kind of hitter that if you threw it 92 miles per hour at me, I'd hit it right back at you"

"The average person – if you had
a situation that hit your family
and you needed to do something,
you would not just go
and take a vacation,
or
you would not do something that's
not related to the task at hand.
But in Washington, that just
seems to be par for the course"

"I don't want to live in a country where the elites like Hillary Clinton do not live under the same laws as the rest of us. She needs to be held to account"

"An approach that phases in congressional term limits reconciles the self-interest of members of Congress with the public's desire to see these changes enacted and gives us the best chance to make term limits a reality"

"Congress cannot be allowed to impose burdens on the American people while relieving its own members of those burdens"

"We must enforce the laws we have on the books, secure our borders, and deny special benefits to illegal immigrants such as in-state tuition rates. This approach is best for American citizens and is fair to those who have taken the time and effort to go through the legal immigration process"

"

Florida is a law-and-order state. We support law enforcement, and Florida shows this not just by words but by deeds.

"My administration works every day to build stronger communities, especially rural ones"

"I'm committed to ensuring Florida continues to be the most veteran-friendly state in the nation, especially for the 1.5 million veterans living in the Sunshine State! Thank you to the Veterans of Foreign Wars for having me at their state convention Saturday night"

"Protecting life does not end with the unborn…I called on the Legislature to promote adoption [and] foster care so all Floridians have a fair chance in life. Florida has 4,000 more licensed caregivers than in 2019 [and] I am proposing additional funds for foster parents"

www.ingramcontent.com/pod-product-compliance
Lightning Source LLC
Chambersburg PA
CBHW052013030426

42334CB00029BA/3209